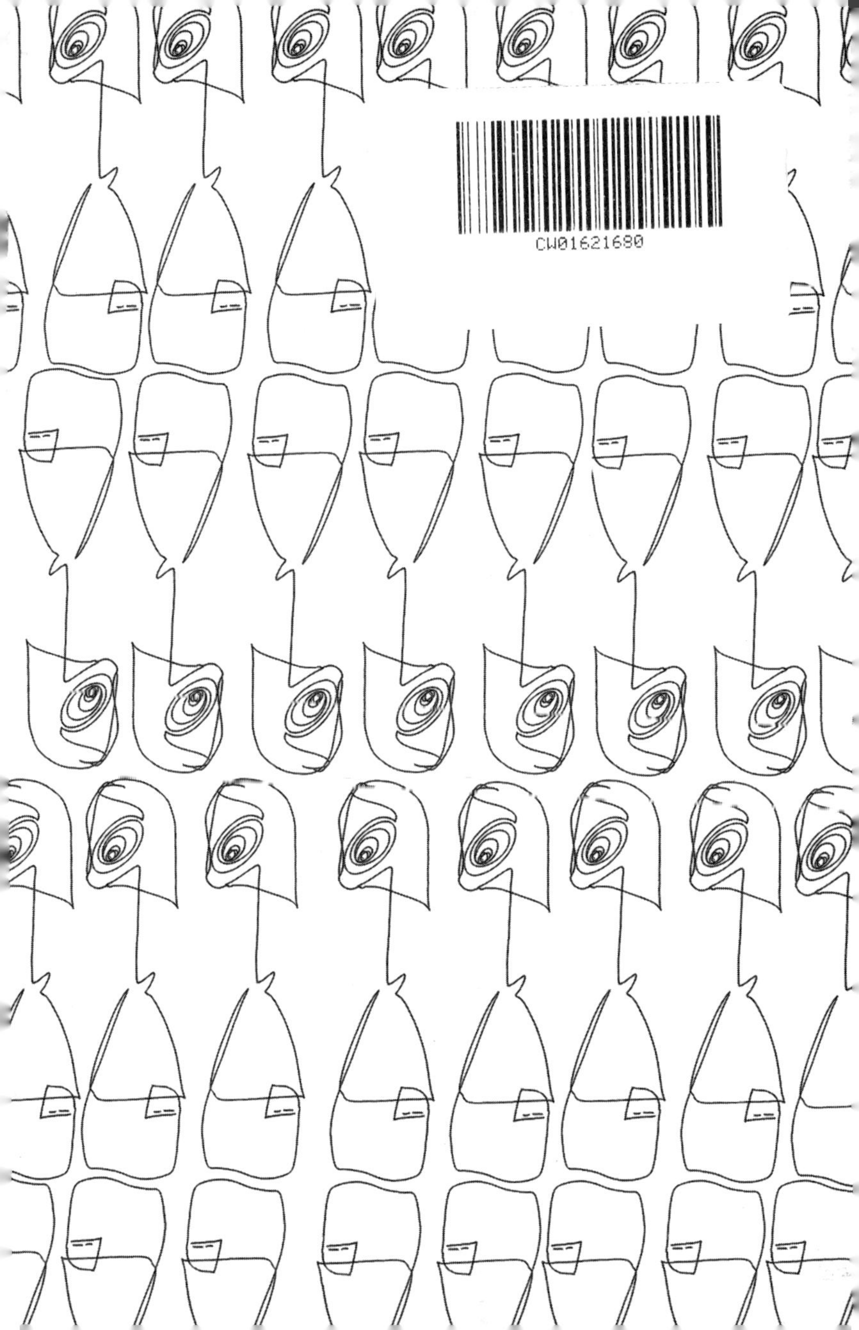

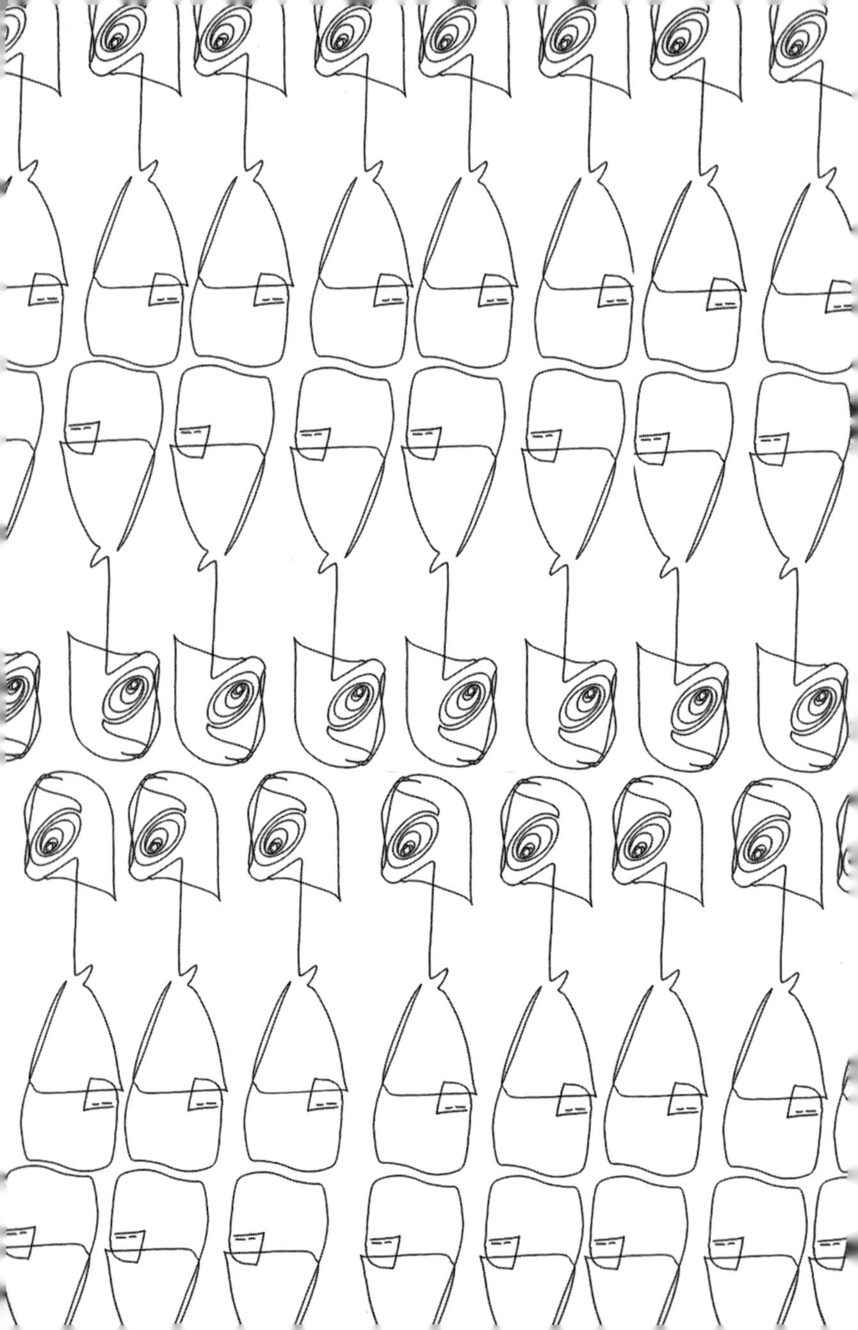

Liberian Pygmy Hippopotamus

Liberian Pygmy Hippopotamus

David Gilbert

Templar Poetry

First Published 2011 by Templar Poetry
Templar Poetry is an imprint of Delamide & Bell

Fenelon House
Kingsbridge Terrace
58 Dale Road, Matlock, Derbyshire
DE4 3NB
www.templarpoetry.co.uk

ISBN 978-1-906285-84-5

A CIP catalogue record of this book is available from the British Library.

Typeset by Pliny
Cover design by James Weir
Printed and bound in India

For Samuel and Adam

Acknowledgements

Acknowledgements are due to the editors of the publications where the following poems have appeared: *Sunderland v Leeds, Unsaid, The Whale, The Walk* (Magma). *The Walk* was also shortlisted in the Bridport Prize (2009); *Then It's Autumn* (The Interpreter's House); *Ward 9* (The Rialto). *Corporate Memory, Sleeping with a Balloon* (The Templar Anthologies: *Buzz* and *Snap* respectively). *Liberian Pygmy Hippopotamus* came third in the Troubadour Open Competition 2009. *Yellow Moth Dead* will appear in the forthcoming Anthology of Contemporary British Prose Poetry (Monson, J [ed], Cinnamon Press, 2011).

I would like to thank all my family and friends who support me in my writing. To my wife Susan particularly, for loving support and late night cups of tea. Special thanks to Robert Vas Dias (and those who have been in his group seminar over the years), Mimi Khalvati (and those in her various workshops) and Laurie Smith (and the Magma family). To all these: Thanks for the quality of your insight, consistent encouragement, passion for words and biscuits.

Contents

Sunderland v Leeds

Friday, my dad sneaked me in
the waiter stole me up
to serve sandwiches to Bremner,
Charlton, Hunter, Lorimer and Giles
bent over a pack of cards, cash
piling to the stars where, breathless,
I wished them luck. And they promised,
promised me, they'd win.

Saturday, I kicked in the door,
scarred by Montgomery's miraculous save,
thousands of red and white scarves,
Stokoe racing across the Wembley turf
in that cheap grey mac
and stupid pork pie hat.

Folding the Sheets

I loved to help my mother in the garden
take down sun- and wind-dried sheets
from the sagging washing line, propped up
in the middle by an old wooden pole.

She'd unclip the clothes pegs one by one,
drop them in an empty terracotta pot
and offer me the edge of a crinkled sheet.
We faced each other: partners in a dance

peering across vast cotton waves,
arms spread out, gripping our corners,
watching each other's every move
bringing together the opposing leaves,

folding, refolding… until she reeled us in
to meet halfway. She kissed my nose
and whisked the bundle out of my hands.
The linen piled high in the wicker basket.

Now I can mirror her with eyes closed,
senses narrowing on the task and line,
opening up to the sound of sparrows
from the branches of the damson tree.

Then it's Autumn

It was hot. It was an oak.
I knew that much
from the Observer Book of Trees.
One straggly branch
hung a little lower than the rest.

Barrie picked up a stick
and poked the duck.
It was quivering and swung
like a slow pendulum –
a wire wrapped round its neck.

I choked back the sick.
They'd only laugh.
The Head called a special assembly.
Someone was eventually
expelled. It got colder. Then

it's Autumn. A Mallard
returns to the pond
whenever the big boys disappear
but refuses the crusts
from my peanut butter sandwiches.

Glass to be Smashed

There's always glass to be smashed.
The ball sailing to the shed
mum open-mouthed with the secateurs.

Or her, red in pearls and high heels
weaving between the guests
with a tray of sherry and canapés.

Or when they divorced.
The men carrying the lithograph
to the white van.

Or later on the ward
Robbie walking to the window
too slowly and deliberately for my liking.

Or when Debbie broke it off.
I'd had it with her aquarium.
Those fucking guppies.

Unsaid

Think of him as a child, the time wasted
as he flipped between chocolate and vanilla,
sauce and flake or neither. Now it's tube, blade
paracetamol or ligature.

He'd haemorrhage beyond recovery
with luck, while waiting for an ambulance,
though more probably, he'd scrape to A&E
and spit gratitude at the consultant.

You care too much to watch him gather dust
in psychiatric corridors. The damage
done at the precipice must be addressed:
Lead him gently to, but leave him at, the bridge

above the Archway Road, or let him down
peacefully on the Northern Line Southbound.

Ward 9

It gets so quiet so quiet I read a lot
turn the pages slowly without rustling
soften crisps between tongue and cheek
whisper in the long white rooms
rummage through carrier bags without a scrunch
hum sonatas diminuendo

they say my heart's percussion requires
toning down my neurones
blaze with some disremembered fire
but they can't know the future can
always catch the past they'll
find out too soon too soon

I hear everything they talk about
in the boiler room the radiators
their feverish swish and rush through
long pipes the valves each morning
that deadly clickety-clack. You hear
the cacophony of leaves outside? The evening
is too loud too loud the rising moon deafening

I would have been happy enough to remain
manager in a shop of silence or curator
archivist librarian gymnast mime or anything
without words – a collector of soothings
perpetual watcher of moons and satellites
but I was so young so young

when I learned to pretend to shout
tasted the shape of *bugger* in my mouth
kept it in began to crave the quiet
till it grew so strong it pinned me down
everything was soon too loud too loud
they keep me here for my own good
you need to go now there's not much time
before the trolley comes round comes round

The Whale

He had to write about it. Two months later
he was dead. We discovered the notebook
and the page where the writing stopped.
We asked around. Others had seen him
rush over the dunes, across the wet sand
and circle the beached body for hours
head down, making notes. He returned each day.
We found descriptions from every possible angle,
how its flanks were contrasting shades,
immense baleen gaping in the heavy gravity,
blowhole exposed to the suffocating atmosphere,
seagulls pecking at its eyes. Page after page
of spidery scrawl charted its decomposition,
how its organs blackened and liquefied.
Lines about the stench, or sound and shape
of the swarms of flies, were crossed out.
Then one day the curtains were drawn.
The doctor said: "He was grey, refusing
to talk or take medicine or lift his pen,
suffering massive and bloody coughing fits".

Corporate Memory

Your old Bechstein lies on the tip
keys cracked, glossy with rain
body rotting, replaced

with yet another harp
in the corner of the office
aching, I like to think, for its strings

to be caressed. The double-bass
before that, the lute, bassoon,
trombone… nothing

seems to satisfy their taste
or can erase the day by day
memory loss. Each instrument

is heaved away before
leaving a carpet mark let alone
a sound. The turn-around time is less

and less. They watch me. I've become
some sort of unpleasant reminder
of *The Orchestra*. When they ask

I say: *I am a music archaeologist*
but I'm not sure I believe it any more.
And it only makes them cross.

Yesterday the boss's young PA
the one with almost perfect pitch
whispered: *You must publish your*

Memoirs of a Pianist.
I shook my head. *It's too late now.*
Mostly I get the day done

proof the manuscripts
eat sandwiches at my desk.
I have a new thermos.

I must return your metronome.
There was something else
I meant to say.

Sleeping with a Balloon

We crept in to find the air
full of whispering
that no rain, no car,
no night bird could explain.

The trees stood stock-still
at odds with this exhalation
like a toy train shoosh
or a thought that clings on.

We let our breath fall
to gather better its sigh,
steady, defiant, like water
heading back towards the hills.

Then the headlights roamed
to sweep the room of shadows
and a momentary fire fixed
the source. We left him there

holding firm in dream.
We prayed it would not burst
and listened into the night
as it shrivelled in his palms.

Via Charing Cross

Fell asleep at Tufnell Park, missed Camden Town, went sailing 'Via Charing Cross', came up at Warren Street. *Well, what the hell,* I thought, turned right, zigzagged unfamiliar streets, walked into a foyer, took a lift to an office that looked OK, sat down at a desk, scanned the in-tray, got up to make a coffee. Don't think anyone noticed till lunchtime, when a guy with blue eyes said: *Hey, Steve. You all right? You look kind of pale. Must have been a rough night.* A woman with glasses said: *Have you done something to your hair? Suits you.* Then she left me with papers to read and file. Drafted a couple of emails, then had a meeting with the senior management team: *Nice tie* said the Chief Executive before we got down to business. *It's been a long day,* I thought later as I wrote an overdue Board Report on Exception Reporting. I hadn't even had lunch. It was getting dark. I put my coat on, headed back to the station, wondered if I'd get home too late or find another one.

The Walk

The day my dad said no to chemo
I went for a walk around the blocks
criss-crossing avenues and old haunts
past the locked-up park head down
dot-to-dot between pubs and bus stops
until it was dusk. A friend rang to ask
how I felt. I said I didn't know.
When we hung up I was stopped
at a driveway's edge staring down
at two pairs of child-size handprints
side-by-side: waving in cement.

Liberian Pygmy Hippopotamus

These days, the Preferred Place of Care
(or PPC) according to academics
is The Home or The Hospice.

Dad prefers to ignore
the finality of words
and officiates from Bed 6 on Ward 11E

summoning us
with parting gifts
as we gather

in comfy chairs provided
by the Project Coordinator for the Patient Pathway (or Matron)
and Betty, the cleaner.

He doesn't want to go home.
He refuses the sweetened pleas of bed managers
to go home. This is home.

Contained by the, at last, certainty
of the rhythmic swish of the morphine pump
and ward rounds.

He swears the profile of a golden lioness
rises glowering from the trees
overlooking The Heath

and the paths where we handfed
Nuthatches, Chaffinches and Robins.
Fewer of them now.

He is more tired today.
I feed him slow spoonfuls
of leek and potato soup

tell him that Samuel
went to the zoo yesterday
held out his hand to touch

the Liberian Pygmy Hippopotamus
almost wiped out by civil war.
That Adam wants to bring it home.

Yellow Moth Dead

You come back tired to find a yellow moth dead in the blue glass on the bathroom sill. Turning the glass to let it fall on your palm you see it is smaller than a 10p coin. For a few seconds you take in thin black lines on its wings like tributaries, pinprick eyes, V of antennae. Then you tip it out of the window into the night and watch for its body disappearing. Afterwards, you turn on the tap, fill the glass with water, pick up the toothbrush and notice the dust shaken from its wings to form a copper silhouette against your lifeline.

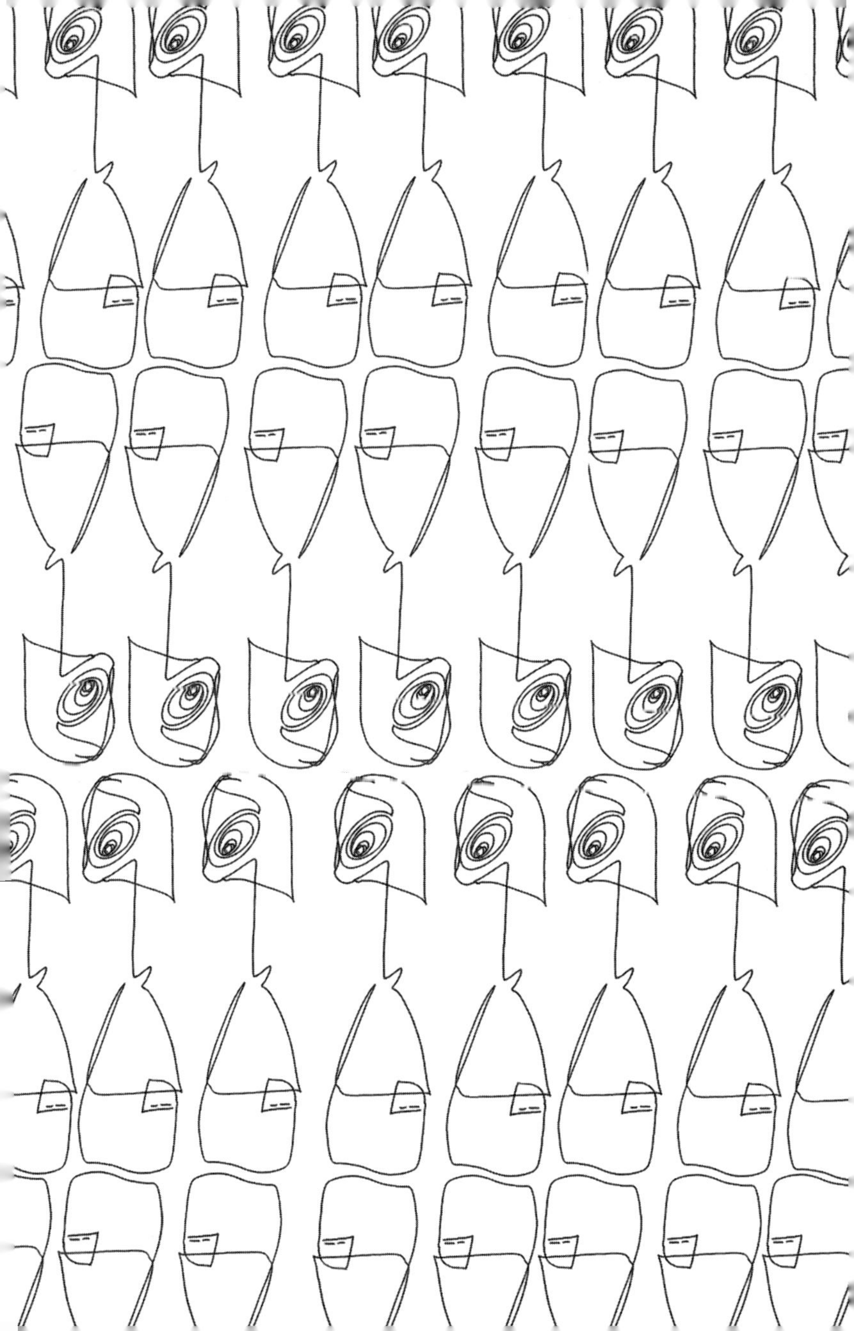

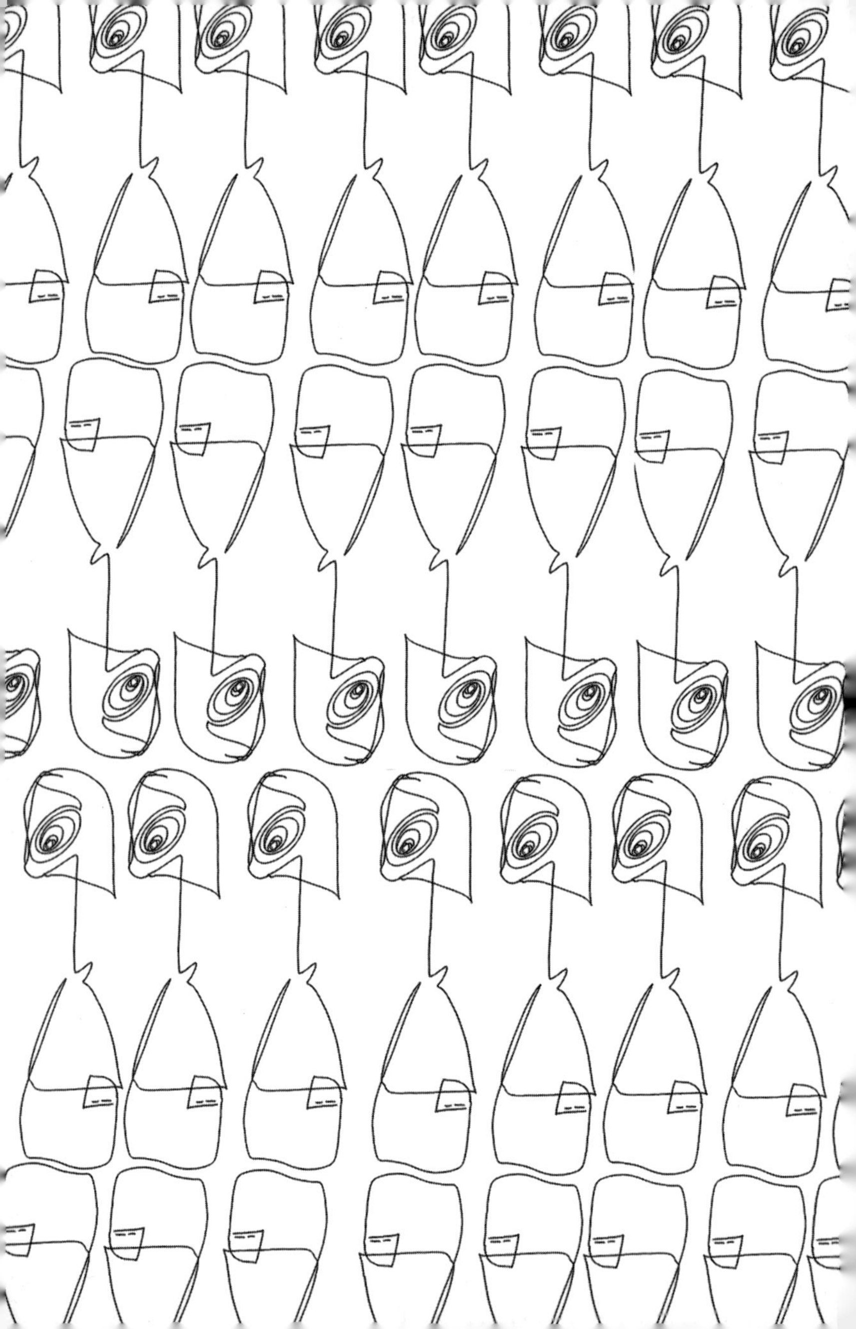